D1144692

EGMONT

We bring stories to life

First published in Great Britain in 2019 by Egmont UK Limited
The Yellow Building, 1 Nicholas Road, London, W11 4AN

Partial content is taken from *Meet Ryan*, published 2018
by Simon Spotlight, an imprint of Simon & Schuster Children's Publishing Division
1230 Avenue of the Americas, New York, New York 10020

ISBN 978 1 4052 9540 6
70640/001
Printed in Italy

ONLINE SAFETY FOR YOUNGER FANS

Spending time online is great fun! Here are a few simple rules to help younger
fans stay safe and keep the internet a great place to spend time.

- Never give out your real name – don't use it as your username
- Never give out any of your personal details
- Never tell anybody which school you go to or how old you are
- Never tell anybody your password except a parent or a guardian
- Be aware that you must be 13 or over to create an account on many sites. Always check the site policy and ask a parent or a guardian for permission before registering
- Always tell a parent or guardian if something is worrying you

Stay safe online. Any website addresses listed in this book are correct at the timeof going to print.
However, Egmont is not responsible for content hosted by third parties. Please be aware that online content
can be subject to change and websites can contain content that is unsuitable for children.
We advise that all children are supervised when using the internet.

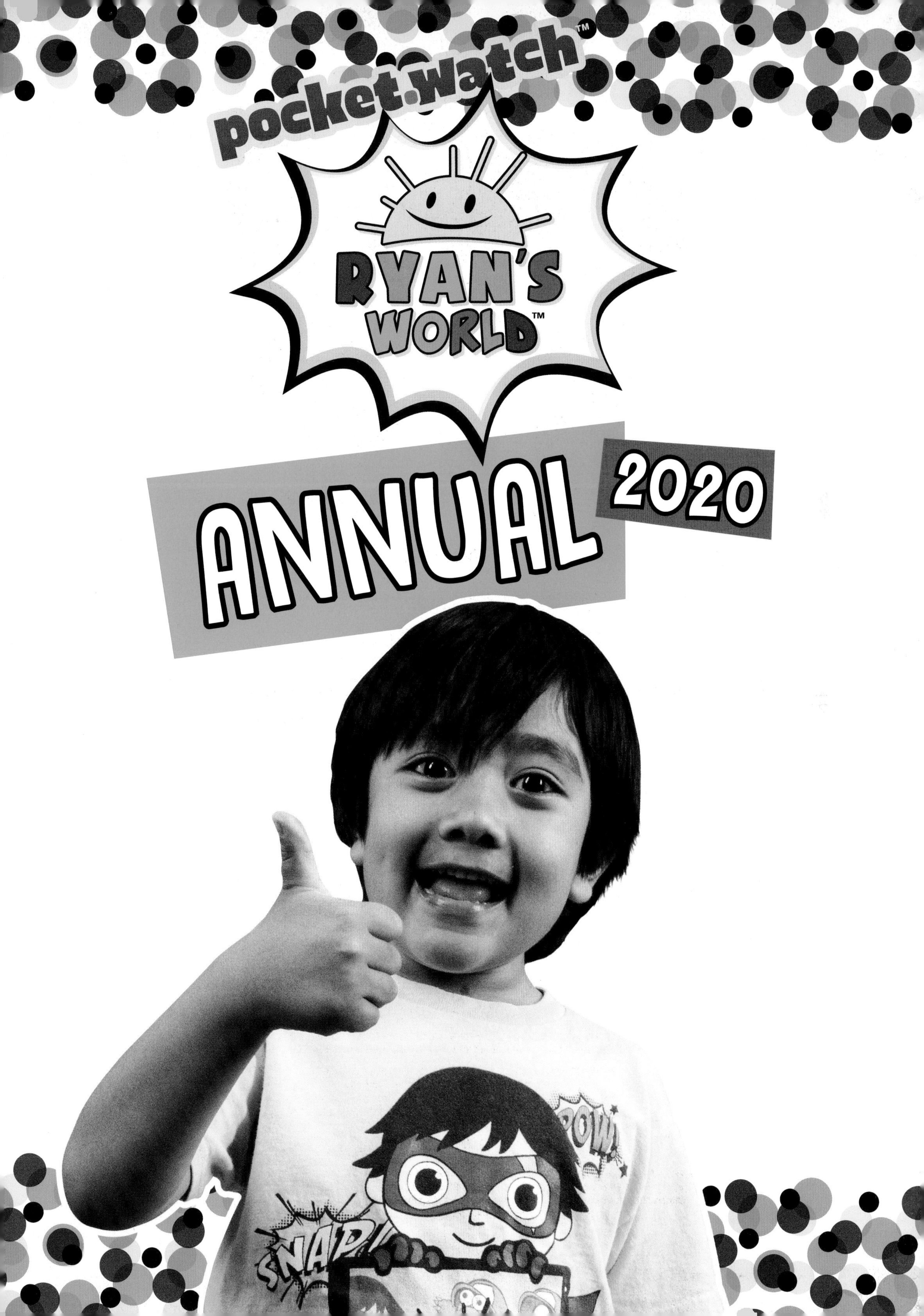
pocket.watch™
RYAN'S WORLD™
ANNUAL 2020
POW!
SNAP!

CONTENTS

This RYAN'S WORLD™ Annual 2020
belongs to:

GUS
R

Hi! I'm
Ryan
from
RYAN'S WORLD™

Welcome to my world. You might have seen some of my videos on my YouTube channel, Ryan's Toys Review. I love to make videos for my fans and friends. Come and take a tour around my world!

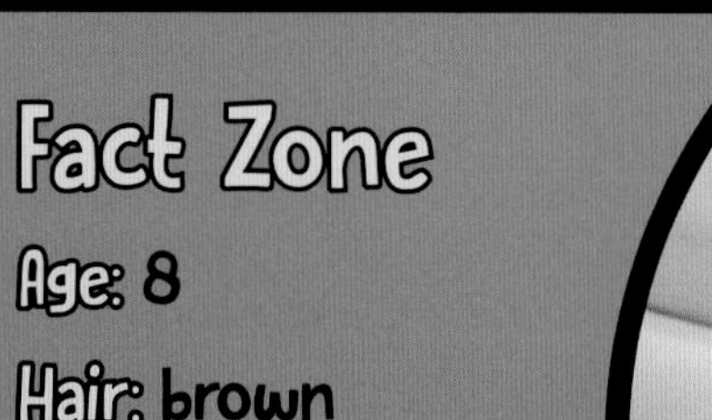

Fact Zone

Age: 8

Hair: brown

Eyes: brown

Hobbies: gaming and playing with toys

Likes: pizza - yum!

Dislikes: scary stories

Other YouTube channels: Ryan's Family Review, VTubers, Combo Panda, Gus the Gummy Gator, the Studio Space

All About You

I'd love to learn all about you and your world. Can you draw a picture of yourself in the frame?

Now fill out your stats and facts!

Fact Zone

Age: ______________________

Hair: ______________________

Eyes: ______________________

Hobbies: ______________________

Likes: ______________________

Dislikes: ______________________

Other: ______________________

My Favourite Things Ever

Check out the bubbles to read all about my favourite things.

Colours:
Neon green and neon blue

Emoji:
Happy face

Football and tennis

Pandas and dinosaurs

Hobbies:
Playing games and drumming

Food:
Pizza and oranges
Subjects:
Maths and music
Ice-cream flavour:
Vanilla
Season:
Summer
Dress-up costume:
Red Titan
Toys:
LEGO blocks and action figures
R

Your Favourite Things Ever

Now it's your turn. Write down all of your favourite things in the bubbles.

Colours: ______________________

Emoji: ______________________

Sport: ______________________

Animals: ______________________

Hobbies: ______________________

Ask your friends about their favourite things!
Food:
Subjects:
Ice-cream flavour:
Season:
Dress-up costume:
Toys:

Surprise Toy Challenge

My mummy and daddy have hidden some green, purple and blue surprise eggs in a giant pool of jelly. Can you help me follow the wibbly wobbly lines to the giant egg, counting the different colours as you go?

How many eggs of each colour did you count?
Point to the answers in the number line.
1 2 3 4 5 6 7 8
When you have counted all the different coloured eggs, turn to page 69 to find out what's inside the giant egg.

Answer on page 68

All About My Family

This is my family. I live with my mummy, daddy and two sisters. You might have seen them in some of my videos.

We love to play together...
... game together...
I love my family!
... go on days out ...
... and have lots of fun.

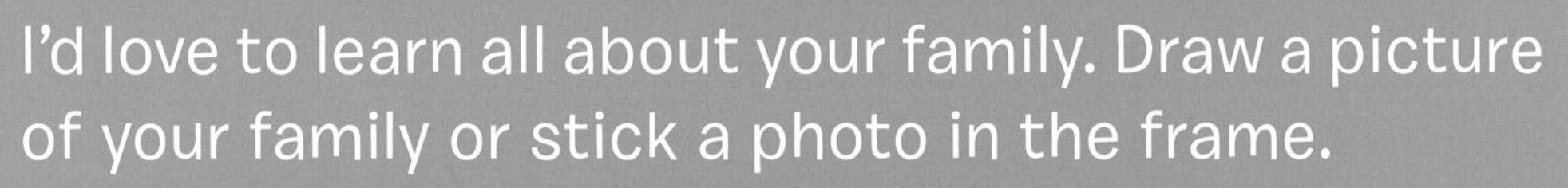

Your Family

I'd love to learn all about your family. Draw a picture of your family or stick a photo in the frame.

Write about three things you love to do together:

1. ______________________________

2. ______________________________

3. ______________________________

Meet My Mummy

This is my mummy. She used to be a science teacher, but now we make videos together. She's doesn't get nervous in front of the camera at all.

Let's have some fun!

Mummy!

FACT ZONE

Hair: Brown

Eyes: Brown

Top skills:

Science experiments

Dream job:

Making animations for kids

Mummy with my VTuber friends!

Silly Spot

My mummy loves being silly, just like me! Can you spot five differences in the second picture? Draw a smile in an emoji each time you find a difference.

1

2

Answer on page 68

Meet My Daddy

This is my daddy. He used to be a structural engineer. He helped to design and build real buildings – so awesome!

I can be shy in front of the camera, but I always have fun!

FACT ZONE

Hair: Brown

Eyes: Brown

Top skills: building anything and everything

Likes: watching nature videos

Daddy!

Build It Up

My daddy helps me build really cool things with blocks. Then he lets me smash them down. **CRASH!**

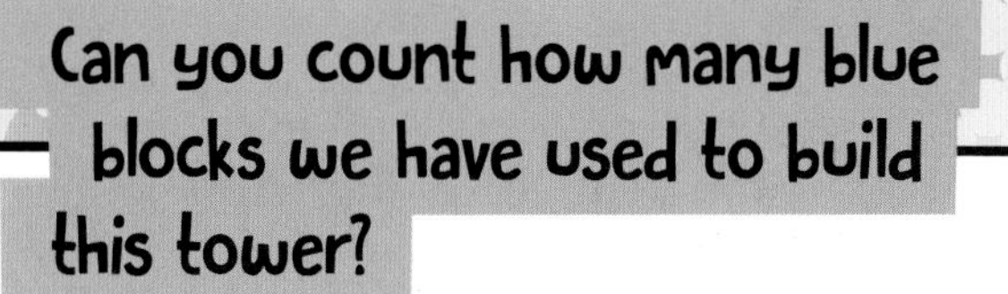

Can you count how many blue blocks we have used to build this tower?

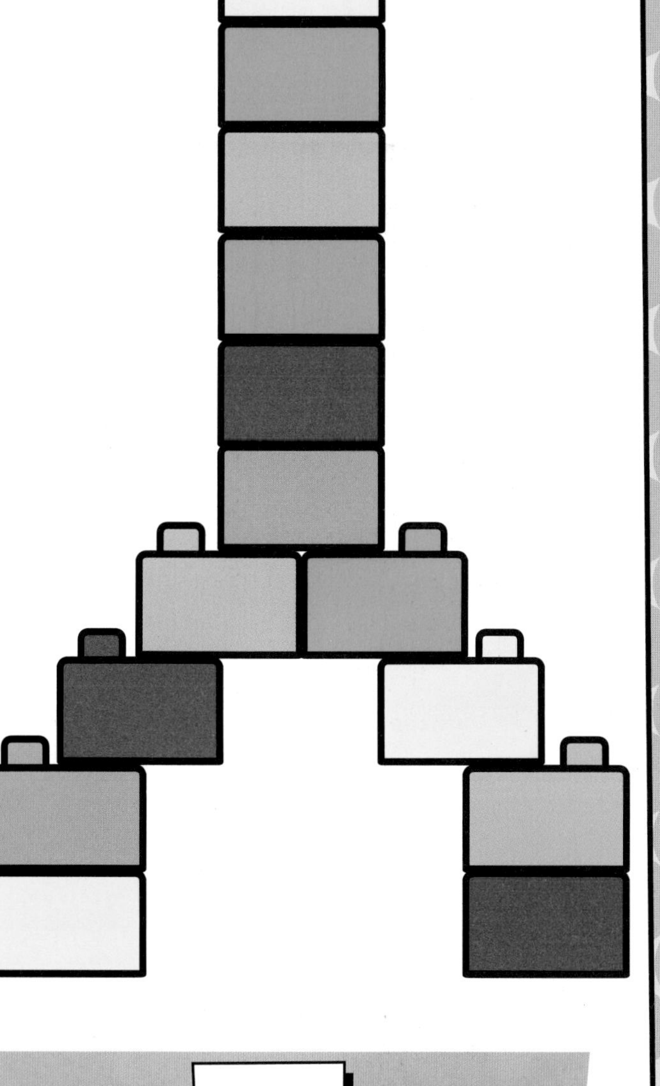

There are ☐ blue blocks.

Now design your own block tower. How many blocks will you use?

Answer on page 68

Alphabet Animals

Do you want to have some messy fun? Follow these easy steps to paint alphabet animals with your hands.

You will need:
*Plates
*Green, blue, orange, black and brown paint
*Paper
*Googly eyes

How to make an amazing alligator

1. Squirt some green paint onto your plate.

2. Now for the messy part! Press the palm of your hand into the paint.

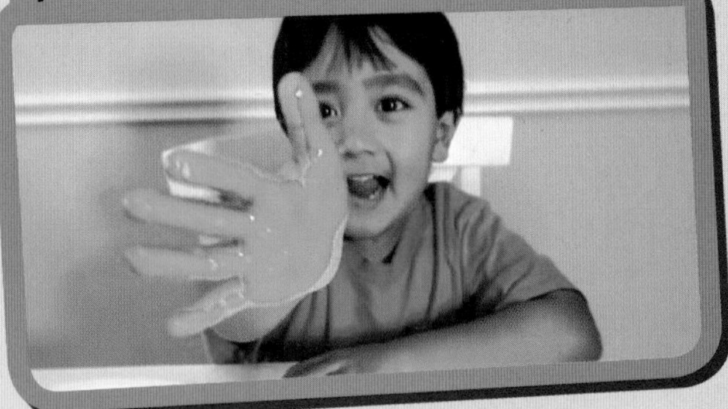

3. Now press your hand down onto your paper. You should see a green handprint.

4. Now turn the paper on its side. Add sharp teeth and stick on some googly eyes.

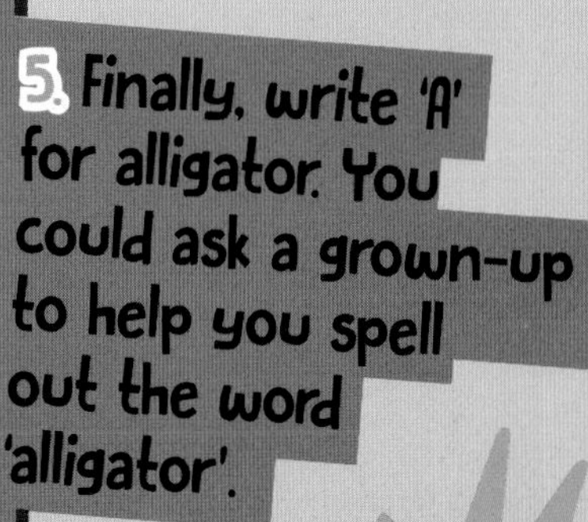

5. Finally, write 'A' for alligator. You could ask a grown-up to help you spell out the word 'alligator'.

How to make a roar-some lion

1. Squirt some orange paint onto a plate.

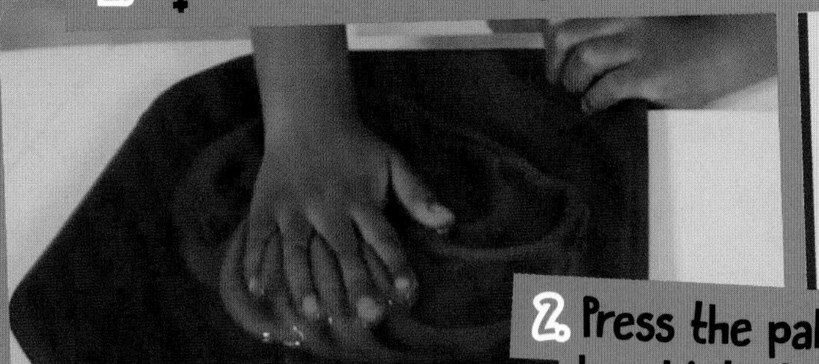

2. Press the palm of your hand into the paint.

3. Now press your hand onto your paper. You should see an orange handprint.

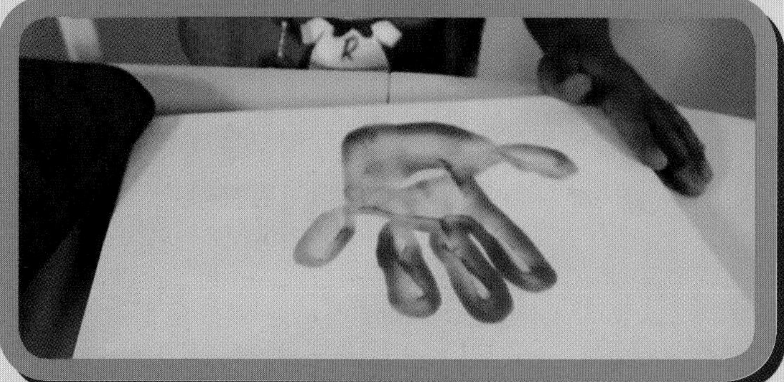

4. Paint on a tail, a mane, a nose and a mouth. Don't forget to stick on your googly eyes!

5. Write 'L' for lion. You could ask a grown-up to help you spell out the word 'lion'.

Meet My Little Sisters

My little sisters are called Emma and Kate. They are twins, which means they were born on the same day. They are full of energy and full of fun!

This is Kate

This is Emma

Lots of people think they look alike, but I can always tell them apart.

Fact Zone

Age: 3

Favourite games: chase and hide-and-seek

Likes: dancing to nursery rhymes and drawing

Hobbies: drawing. They even have their own YouTube channel called EK Doodles

Being a big brother is the best!

Double Trouble

Check out these photos of me and the twins going for a ride. **Whee!**
The photos might all look the same, but one is different. Can you spot the odd one out?

MY SISTERS!

Answer on page 68

My School Day

Read along to find out all about my school day. When you see a picture, join in and say the word out loud.

School today! My  wakes me up early. **YAWN!**

I put on my , brush my teeth and eat breakfast. The  always make a mess but I try to keep my school  clean. We usually have cereal for breakfast – yum! Now I am ready to go. See you soon, !

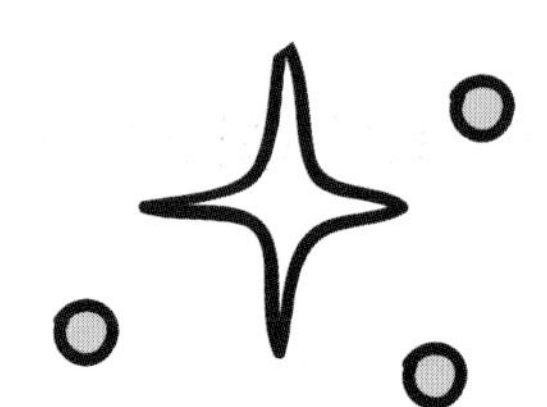

 drives me to school. I have maths class all morning, and then it's lunch. I buy 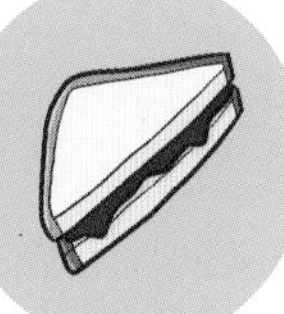 and some milk. I like ketchup 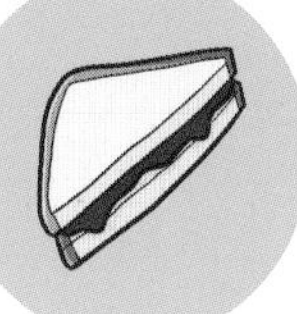 best.

In science class we learn about a  erupting. Did you know hot lava spills down a  when it erupts? **Boom!** I tell my class all about the experiment I did when I made my own exploding .

Then I have geography class, where I learn all about the  . Today I get to draw a map of Japan, which is my favourite country in the whole  . When I am older, I hope I get to travel the  with my family.

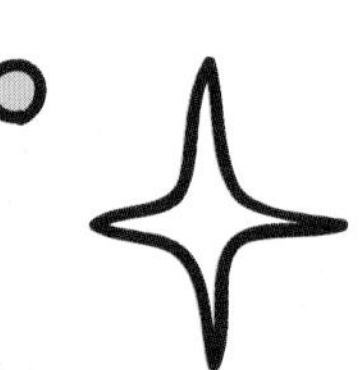

After school,  picks me up and I go to  class. I get to play the drums and guitar. Fast  is my favourite. I have to dance if I hear some good !

After  class it's time for  to take me back home to see daddy and the .

What a busy day!

If you want to find out what I do when I get home from school, turn to page 60...

Making My Videos

With the help of my family, I have posted more than 1000 videos on YouTube. Do you want to find out more about how we do it? Check out this video quiz.

Q: What are your videos about?

A: Lots of my videos are about playing with toys. I love finding toys in surprise eggs. I also do science experiments, crafts, gaming and singing.

Q: What is the best place you have found a surprise toy?

A: In ball pools, mazes, inflatable slides ... it's too hard to choose one!

Q: When do you film your videos?

A: Mostly at weekends, when my sisters are napping.

Q: When did you start making your videos?

A: When I was three years old.

Q: What do you love about making videos?

A: I get to play with my favourite toys, have fun with my family and make kids laugh all over the world.

Q: Have you won any awards for your videos?

A: Yes! I won a Silver Play Button trophy when I got 100,000 subscribers, a Gold Play Button trophy when I got 1 million subscribers and a Diamond Play Button for 10 million subscribers.

Q: Who stars in your videos?

A: My mummy, daddy and twin sisters. I also have my VTubers who help me out with my gaming videos.

Q: Where do you film the gaming videos for your VTubers channel?

A: We have a special gaming room in my house with a giant computer, a TV, a Wii U, a PlayStation 4 and more!

Q: Have you got any advice for anyone making videos?

A: Yes! Do something you love, ask your family for help and don't worry if something goes wrong. That's all part of the fun!

My Most-Watched Videos

I love making all my videos, but my fans definitely have some favourites. Let's countdown my top 5 most-watched videos EVVEE**ERRRRRR!**

5 Balloon Pop Surprise Toys Challenge

258,981,732 views

I got to splash around in a giant inflatable pool filled with balls and balloons. I popped the balloons to find surprise cars and toy figures hidden inside.

4 Thomas and Friends Giant Ball Pits with Egg Surprise Toys

315,284,208 views

This was so cool because I got to roll, run and jump on tons of balls and an inflatable crocodile. The best bit was finding the egg surprise with a toy car inside.

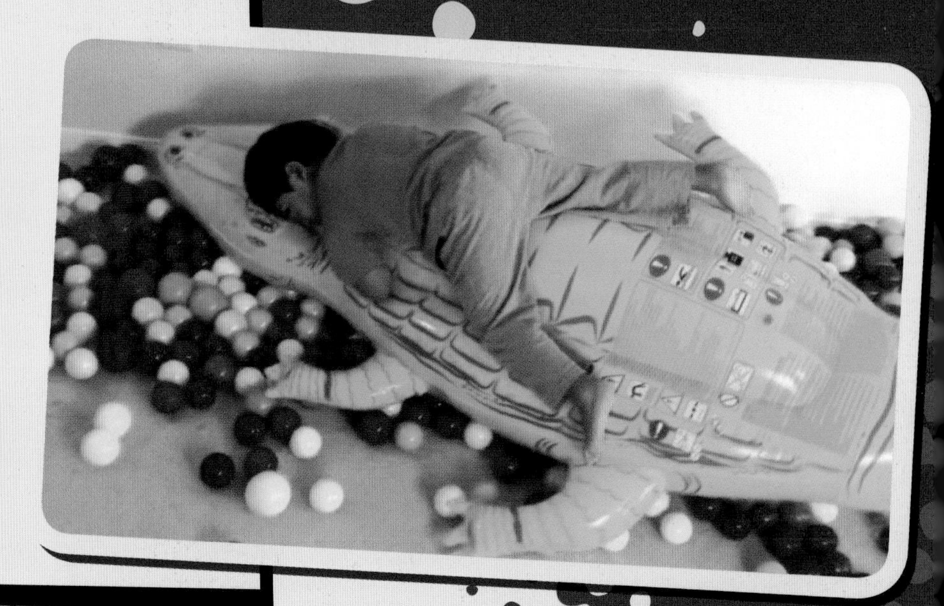

3 Indoor Playground with Giant Inflatable Slides

348,327,623 views

Woah! Those giant slides were so much fun. I loved playing crashes with the trikes and diving in the ball pits. This was an awesome video to make.

2 Giant Lightning McQueen Egg Surprise

949,844,108 views

My second most-viewed video had a giant egg filled with over 100 cars. There were so many surprises to find, it took me forever to get them all out!

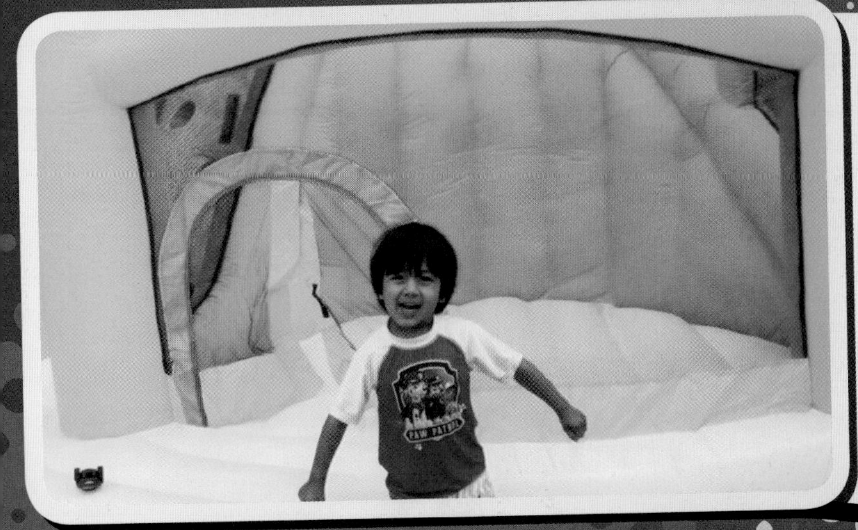

1 Huge Eggs Surprise Toy Challenge

1,741,412,458 views

My most-watched video EVER! I got to climb around a huge inflatable water slide and collect eggs. All the eggs had the most AMAZING surprises hidden inside.

And that's it! Hope you enjoyed reading about them.

Music Magic

I don't just make videos about toys, I make music videos too. I love to dance and sing.

Why don't you put on your favourite song and join in with our actions? Once you remember the actions in order, you can perform a super-silly Ryan's World dance routine!

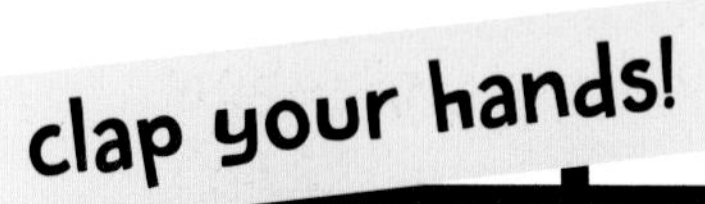
clap your hands!

stretch your arms

jump up high

do a spin

drive a car

wiggle your hips

ninja move!

GOT IT?

You could add some of your own moves too!

Matching Pair

Phew! All that dancing has made me tired. I think it is time for a game.

Only two of these photos of me playing the keyboard match exactly. Can you find the matching pair?

Answer on page 68

Amazing Facts

My mummy always says I am curious, and I really am! Check out some cool facts I have learned from doing some of my videos.

Super Size

Did you know that the biggest shark is the world is the whale shark? It can grow to more than 40 feet. That's longer than a school bus!

Crazy Colours

Did you know that when the sun shines on rain droplets in the sky, the light bends and makes a rainbow. That is awesome!

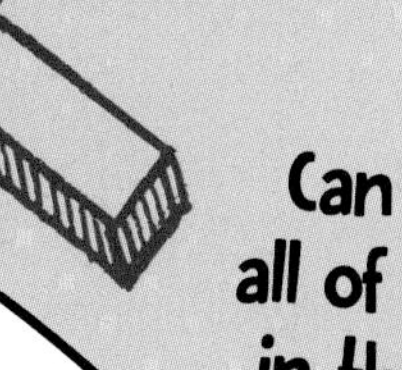

Colour in the rainbow!

Can you name all of the colours in the rainbow?

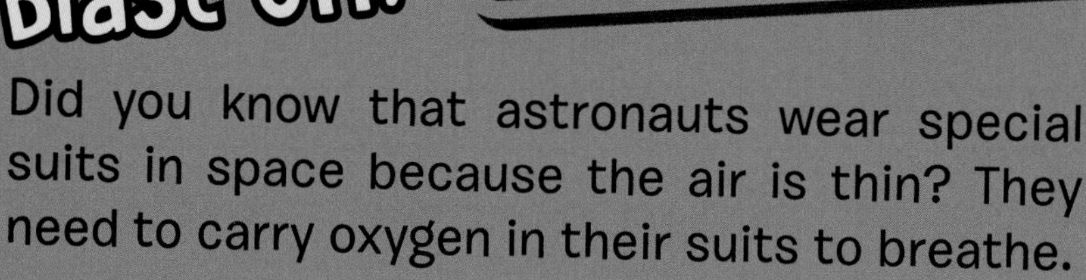

Blast Off!

Did you know that astronauts wear special suits in space because the air is thin? They need to carry oxygen in their suits to breathe.

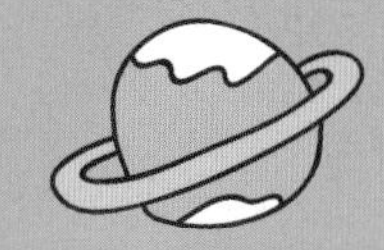

Astro Cat

Did you know that a cat has travelled into space? A kitty was sent up to the stars in 1963. When she came back down to Earth, she was purr-fectly happy!

Snack Time

Did you know that pandas eat bamboo for up to 12 hours a day? That's a lot of munching!

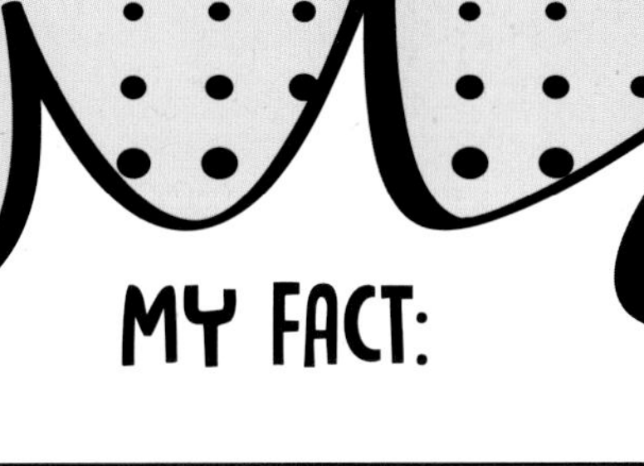

Do you know any cool facts about our world? Tell somebody in your family your favourite fact.

MY FACT:

____

____

____

3, 2, 1 ... Race!

Let's go!

Vroom! Vroom! Use your finger to race through the game to catch up with my VTuber friends. Collect up all the suns along the way.

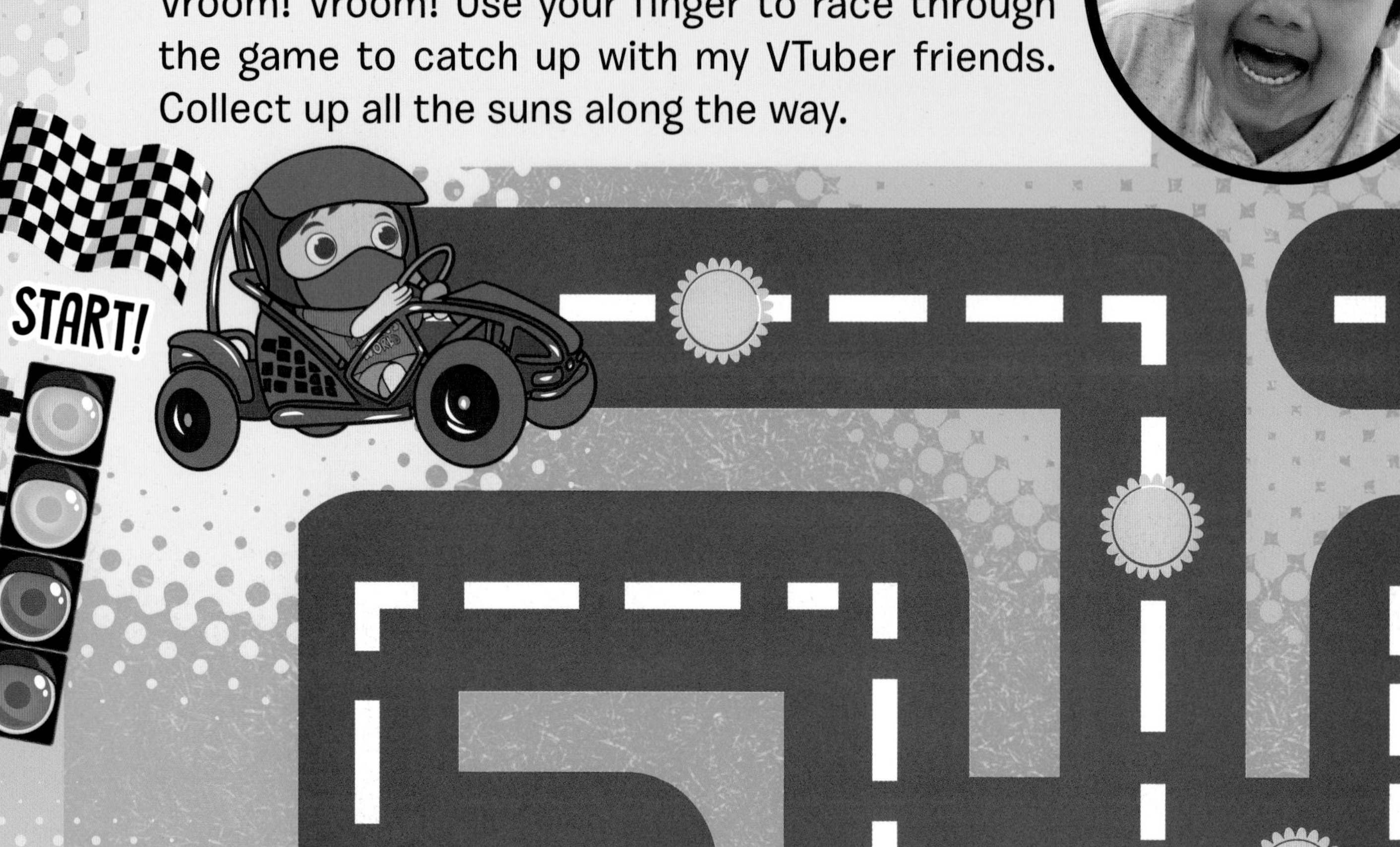

Zoooooooom!
Keep going, you are winning!

How many suns did you collect?

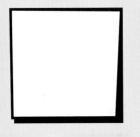

Answer on page 68

Super Friends

One of the best parts of being on YouTube is my fans and making new friends.

Awesome Fans

Hi!

Sometimes I meet fans in the playground. I love it when they say "hi" because I feel like I have made a new friend.

Finding Friends

Let's play!

Making new friends is so cool, but sometimes it's hard to know what to do. Check out my top 5 tips on how to make friends wherever you go.

1. Say "hi"!
2. Tell them your name.
3. Ask them if they'd like to play.
4. Ask them about the things they like.
5. Tell them about your favourite things.

Why don't you try out my tips next time you are at the playground?

A fan once came up to me and said "How are you here? I just saw you on my iPad!". That was so funny. You might watch me on your screen but in real life I'm just a regular kid, like you!

Colour Splash

My VTuber friends are all different colours. Can you draw lines to link up each of the VTubers to their matching paint splats?

I am orange

I am red

I am green

I am blue

I am pink

Answer on page 69

My Dream Job

I love gaming so much, I want to be a game developer when I grow up. Then I can spend all day playing video games with my VTuber friends!

Can you spot FIVE differences between these two pictures?

I hope I'm still making YouTube videos when I'm older, too!

Answer on page 69

Your Dream Job

What would you love to be when you grow up? Write your top 3 dream jobs in the space below.

When I grow up, I want to be...

1.

2.

3.

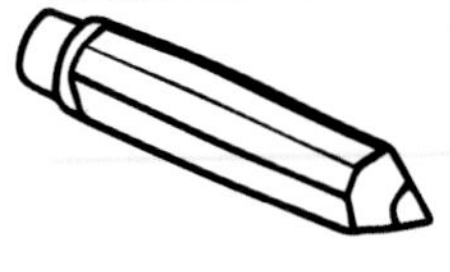

Now draw a picture of yourself doing one of your dream jobs!

Would You Rather...

I love playing a game called 'Would You Rather...' with my mum. Would you like to play along? Just pick your favourite answers – easy-peasy!

Would you rather...
be a pirate
OR
be a ninja?
be able to fly
OR
make yourself invisible?
Welcome home!
live in a giant peach
OR
in a giant shoe?

live somewhere super cold

OR

somewhere super hot?

have stinky feet

OR

bad breath?

be super strong

OR

be super fast?

be the world's best skateboarder

OR

be the world's best surfer?

live in space

OR

under the sea?

be a shark

OR

be a hawk

Match Me Up

Are you ready to play an awesome game to test your brain power? Follow the super easy instructions to play along.

HOW TO PLAY:

1. You will need two players.
2. Ask a grown-up to cut out little pieces of paper to cover up each picture.

3. When all of the pictures are covered, the first player picks up a piece of paper from each side of the book.
4. If your pictures match, keep the pieces of paper. If they don't, put the paper back and it is the second player's turn.
5. The player with the most pieces of paper at the end of the game, wins!

MEET THE VTUBERS!
VTUBERS

Red Titan

Did you know I can transform into a superhero called Red Titan on my VTubers channel?

I am super speedy and super strong ... I can lift anything!

FACT ZONE

Costume: red cape and red mask

Favourite game: Tag with Ryan from Ryan's World

Superpower: strong enough to break through walls, KAPOW!

Speed rating: 10/10. The ultimate speed seeker.

Let's race!

474
17835

WOW!

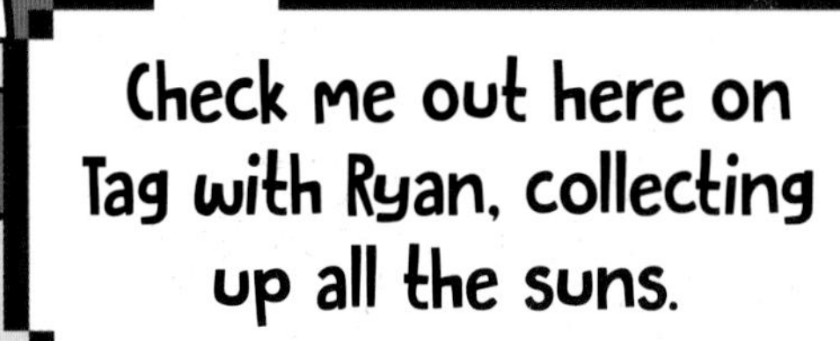
Check me out here on Tag with Ryan, collecting up all the suns.

Colour Combos

Colour key:

Red Yellow Black

Use the key to colour in Red Titan!

Peck

Say hi to Peck! Kind and super smart, this little penguin has a BIG brain. He spends his time studying, gaming and playing with his VTuber friends.

FACT ZONE

Lives: South Pole

Likes: ice pops – yum!

Ambition: to be a scientist

Fun fact: he loves to go SQUAWK!

Check out Peck playing on VTubers from his icy home. Brrrrrr, that's a lot of ice!

Big Gil

Say hi to Big Gil! He might be big and his teeth might be sharp, but there's no need to be scared of this friendly shark. Big Gil loves to play and have lots of fun.

FACT ZONE

Lives: underwater

Likes: gaming, swimming and hanging out with the VTubers

Colour: blue

Favourite games: Roblox and Mario Kart

Colour Combos

Colour key Big Gil:

Colour in these awesome VTubers!

Colour key Peck:

Combo Panda

Say hi to Combo Panda! Leader of the Combo Crew, he is loud, proud and a totally pro gamer. He has his own YouTube channel, too.

Combo-bunga! It's showtime!
ZAP!

FACT ZONE

Likes: chasing VTubers and doing ninja kicks

Dislikes: losing games

Ambition: to have the whole world in his Combo Crew!

Combo Panda YouTube subscribers: 837,630

Check out Combo chasing me in Tag with Ryan.
POW!
205
6552

Colour Combos

Colour key:

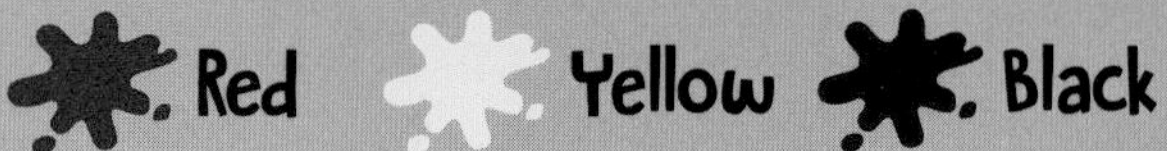

Red

Yellow

Black

Doodle in your favourite gaming character, so Combo has somebody to chase.

MEET THE VTUBERS!
VTUBERS
Gus the Gummy Gator
Say hi to Gus! He is an awesome alligator who can sometimes do crazy and silly things, but he is full of fun and adventure.
Give me that yummy gummy!
FACT ZONE
Likes: having wild adventures with the VTubers
Favourite food: gummy sweets
Best friend: Moe
Gus the Gummy Gator YouTube subscribers: 725,777
GUS
GUS
D
I have my own YouTube channel - come and check out my adventures!
GUS the Gummy Gator

Colour Combos

Colour key:

 Red  Yellow Green

Colour in this gummy-mad gator!

Alpha Lexa

Say hi to Alpha Lexa! She is a super cool gamer girl who loves to beat Combo Panda at everything. Alpha wants to show the world that girls ROCK!

FACT ZONE

Likes: gaming, fashion and baking cookies

Dislikes: losing to Combo Panda

Favourite colour: pink, pink, pink!

Favourite pizza topping: pineapples and tuna

Colour Combos

Colour key:

Blue Pink Green Light Pink

Use the key to colour in this great gamer!

Moe

Say hi to Moe! He is from the faraway planet, Moetopia, but he loves living here on Earth. He always finds clever ways to get out of trouble.

Give me that yummy gummy!

FACT ZONE

Language: an unknown language from Outer Space

Likes: going on adventures and building with blocks

Dislikes: making mistakes

Best friend: Gus the Gummy Gator

This is Moetopia, Moe's home. So cool!

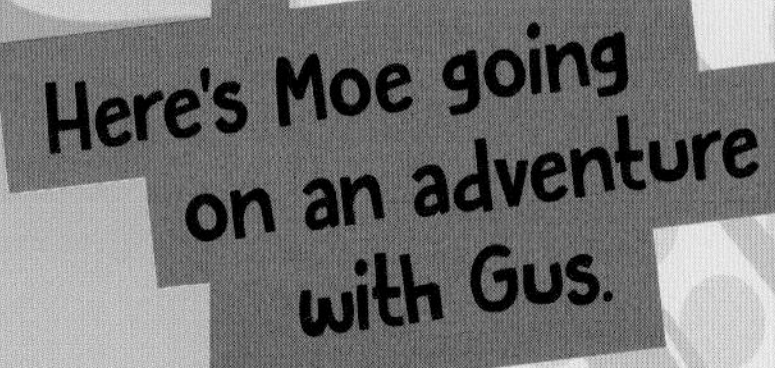

Here's Moe going on an adventure with Gus.

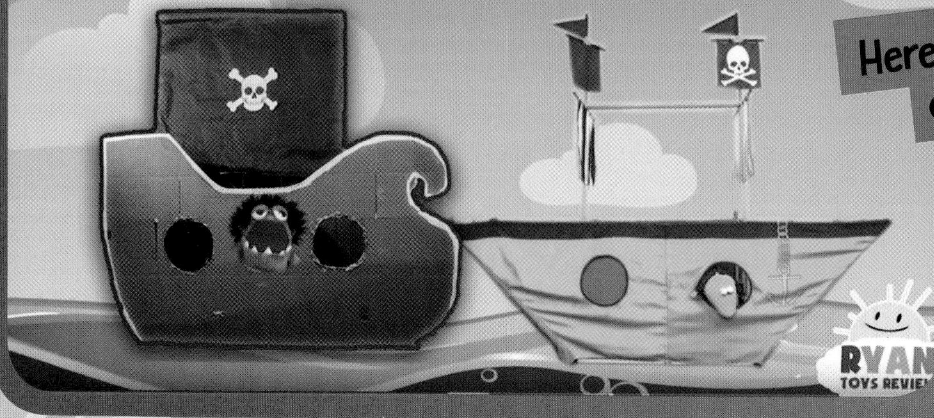

Colour Combos

Colour key:

Can you invent a new planet for Moe to visit? Draw it here.

What's your planet called?

After School

Read along to find out what I do when I get home from school. When you see a picture, join in and say the word out loud.

When I get home from school, I play with my

 and do some drawing. This is the best

part of the day. I share my  with the

 so we can all play together.

I sit down to eat dinner with my mummy, 

 and the  . Tonight, we are having

 – yippee! I love it when we have 

because it's my favourite food.

After dinner, I quickly tidy up my .

I have made a big mess and I don't want

Mummy and  to be cross.

Going in the  is always fun in our house.

Tonight, I get to take my  in the  and play crashes and splashes with my monster trucks.

After my ,  plays a video game with me. I beat him at Tag on Ryan's World and I get my highest score!

I start to feel tired. YAWN! It's nearly time for . makes me and the 

a glass of warm  . I have  every day. After  ,  reads me a story

in  . I choose one about a space 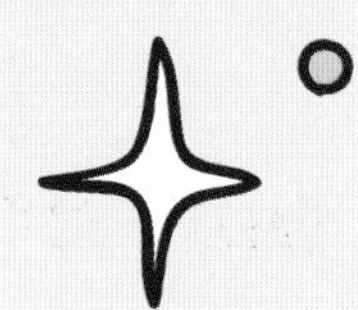

adventure. Goodnight, everyone!

Zzzzzzzzzzzzzzz.

Circle the answers below that would make a perfect day for you.

School OR home

Pizza OR pasta

Playing video games OR playing with toys

Sunny OR rainy

Staying in OR playing out

Movie OR reading

Make Your Own Twisty Tracks

Are you ready for some twisty-turny, messy play? Follow these easy instructions to make super-cool car tracks in all colours of the rainbow.

You will need:

* A giant piece of paper or a roll of paper
* Bowls or plates of different-coloured paint
* Some toy cars and trucks. Try to use vehicles with different patterns on the wheels

What to do:

1. Lay out your paper on a flat surface.
2. Then dip the wheels of a vehicle in one of the paint colours.
3. Race your vehicle around the paper to make twisty tracks.
4. Now pick up another vehicle and get racing with paint again! Try to dip each vehicle into a different paint colour so you get a whole rainbow of tyre tracks.

3... 2... 1... race!

TOP TIP
Set up your paper outside because this could get messy!

TIDY UP!
Ask an adult to help you wash your vehicles in warm, soapy water when you've finished.

TEST IT!

Let's see how much you remember your tour around my world. Take this quiz and then add up your scores. All the answers are hidden in this book.

1. What planet is Moe from?
   a. Moetopia
   b. Mars
   c. Gametopia

2. What superhero does Ryan turn into?
   a. Gus the Gummy Gator
   b. Red Viper
   c. Red Titan

3. What are Ryan's favourite animals?
   a. dinosaurs and pandas
   b. snakes and spiders
   c. monkeys and frogs

4. What are Ryan's virtual friends called?
   a. MeTubers
   b. VTubers
   c. ZzzzzTubers

5. Where does Ryan find lots of his surprise toys?
   a. hidden inside pizza
   b. hidden inside space rockets
   c. hidden inside eggs

6. What does Ryan want to do when he grows up?
   a. a clown
   b. a games developer
   c. a TV presenter

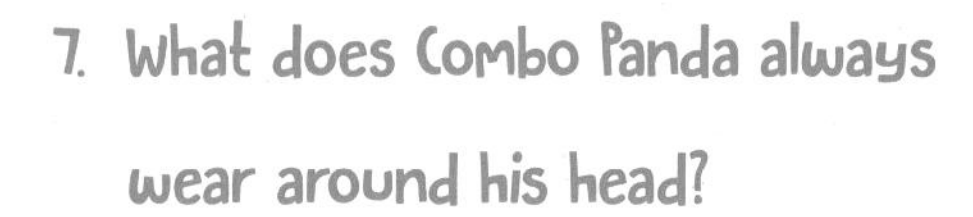

7. What does Combo Panda always wear around his head?
   a. a hat
   b. a hairband
   c. headphones

8. How many videos has Ryan made?
   a. 100
   b. 1000
   c. 1000000

9. Before making videos, what job did Ryan's mummy have?
   a. a science teacher
   b. a music teacher
   c. a chef

10. What animal is Alpha Lexa?
   a. a snail
   b. a dog
   c. a cat

How did you score?

0-3 points
Well done for trying! You are an awesome fan for trying your best.

4-6 points
Cool score. Your memory is out of this world!

7-10 points
Woah, that's a really high score. You are the champion!

Answers on page 69

Answers

Page 14 **Surprise Toy Challenge**

1) There are 4 blue eggs.

2) There are 6 purple eggs.

3) There are 5 green eggs.

Page 19 **Silly Spot**

Page 21 **Build It Up**

There are 3 blue blocks.

Page 25 **Double Trouble**

The odd one out is picture 3.

Page 35 **Matching Pair**

The matching photos are 4 and 5.

Page 39 **3, 2, 1 Race!**

You collected 8 suns.

Page 41 **Colour Splash**

Colour Splash

My VTuber friends are all different colours. Can you draw lines to link up each of the VTubers to their matching paint splats?

I am orange

I am red

I am green

I am blue

I am pink

41

Page 42 **My Dream Job**

Page 66 **Test It!**

1. Moetopia.
2. Red Titan.
3. Dinosaurs and pandas.
4. VTubers.
5. Hidden inside eggs.
6. A games developer.
7. Headphones.
8. 1000.
9. A science teacher.
10. A cat.

You've found your surprise toy!